21st Century Skills Library

REAL WORLD SCIENCE
SOIL

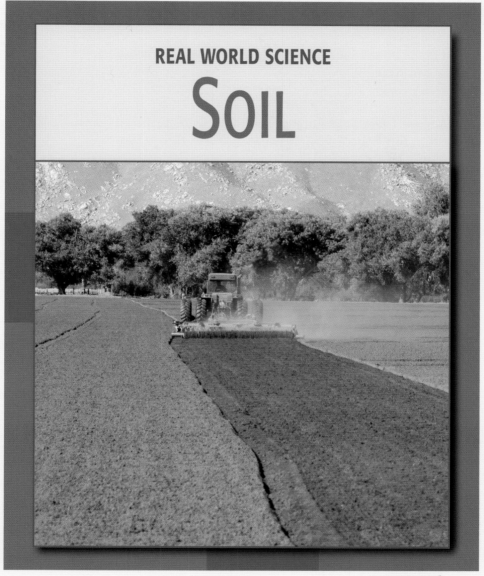

Katie Sharp

Cherry Lake Publishing
Ann Arbor, Michigan

CHERRY LAKE
Publishing

Published in the United States of America by Cherry Lake Publishing
Ann Arbor, Michigan
www.cherrylakepublishing.com

Content Adviser: Laura Graceffa, middle school science teacher; BA degree in science, Vassar College; MA degrees in science and education, Brown University

Photo Credits: Cover and page 1, © Shutterstock; page 4, © Curtis Barnard/Shutterstock; page 7, © Paknyushcha/Shutterstock; page 8, © Clarence Bowman/Shutterstock; page 9, © guidocava/Shutterstock; page 10, Edward Kinsman/Photo Researchers, Inc.; page 12, Sinclair Stammers/Photo Researchers, Inc.; page 14, © Ramunas Bruzas/Shutterstock; page 17, Maury Aaseng; page 19, USDA/Photo Researchers, Inc.; page 21, Fletcher & Bayliss/Photo Researchers, Inc.; page 23, © Shutterstock; page 24, Wayne Lawlor/Photo Researchers, Inc.; page 25, Kenneth Murray/Photo Researchers, Inc.; page 27, © Lilac Mountain/Shutterstock

Library of Congress Cataloging-in-Publication Data

Sharp, Katie John.
Soil / by Katie Sharp.
  p. cm.—(Real world science)
Includes index.
ISBN-13: 978-1-60279-464-1
ISBN-10: 1-60279-464-2
1. Soils—Juvenile literature. I. Title. II. Series.

S591.3.S53 2009
631.4—dc22   2008049661

Cherry Lake Publishing would like to acknowledge the work of
The Partnership for 21st Century Skills.
Please visit www.21stcenturyskills.org for more information.

TABLE OF CONTENTS

CHAPTER ONE

THE DIRT ON SOIL

Plants need soil to grow and thrive.

Everyone knows that people and animals need water and air to live. But did you know that soil is just as important? Without soil there could be no life.

Soil is the outermost layer of the earth. Plants come to life and grow in soil. In turn, people and animals rely on plants for food and **oxygen**. Soil also provides a home to billions of living things.

If you plant a seed in soil, it will likely soon burst through the ground. That's because soil has what plants need to sprout and grow: **nutrients**, water, and oxygen.

Your body needs vitamins and minerals to grow. Plants need certain nutrients, too. For instance, plants need nitrogen, potassium, and calcium. Soil contains all of these nutrients and more. Unlike you, however, plants cannot eat nutrients. Instead they have to absorb, or suck them up, through their roots.

But nutrients are too big to simply move into the roots. They first must dissolve, or break down, in water. Once a plant's roots absorb nutrient-rich

The secrets of the past often lie hidden in the soil. In June 2008 scientists unearthed a large group of dinosaur bones, or fossils. The bones had been hidden beneath the soil of southwestern Utah for 150 million years. The bones came from at least four plant-eating dinosaurs and two meat eaters. From these and other fossil finds, scientists can learn about life on earth millions of years ago.

water from the soil, the water travels all through the plant. It delivers the nutrients to the plant's different parts. The water and nutrients help the plant grow.

REAL WORLD SCIENCE CHALLENGE

With a toothpick, poke holes in the bottom of two paper cups. Fill each cup with soil (from your yard or a bag of potting soil). Then plant a bean seed or two in the soil. Set the cups in a sunny place and keep the soil moist. Next, place a damp paper towel in each of two small plastic containers or bowls. Place a bean seed or two on each towel. Then cover the seeds with another damp paper towel. Place the containers next to the cups and keep the towels damp. Observe the seeds every day for two weeks. Keep a record of any changes. What did you see after the first week? What did you see after the second week? Which seeds grew best?

(Turn to page 29 for the answer)

Another ingredient of soil is oxygen. Plants absorb oxygen in the soil through their roots. The plants need this oxygen to produce energy. They use this energy to function and grow.

Soil provides food and a home for animals such as this earthworm.

Plants are important to other living things because they supply them with oxygen and food. Without plants, humans and animals would not have air to breathe. And fruits and vegetables come from plants. Cows graze on grass and pigs eat corn. In turn, many people eat the meat of these animals.

But without plants, people would not have meat to eat. And without soil, there would be no plants. When you eat plants and the meat of animals that eat plants, your body takes in the nutrients that those plants absorbed from soil.

Groundhogs make their homes in the soil.

Soil is important to many living things for another reason. Many creatures live at least part of their lives in soil. Some you know, such as rabbits, worms, and ants. But many you may not know. These include **bacteria**, **fungi**, and insects.

With billions of **organisms** in the soil, there is more life within soil than above it. And all of these life forms play a part in how soil forms.

CHAPTER TWO

HOW SOIL FORMS

Pieces of rock, bits of rotting plants, air, and water combine to make soil.

Earth is covered with different types of soil. The ocean floor has wet, sandy soil. Rich farmland soil is dark and moist. And deserts have a blanket of dry, sandy soil. No matter where it is or what it looks like, soil always has the same ingredients. All soil is made up of pieces of rock, bits of plant and animal matter, air, and water.

Wind and water erosion have sculpted a rocky hill near Lake Ontario.

The main ingredient in all soil is rock. Scientists call the rock that soil

comes from **parent material**. Look closely at a handful of soil. You will

see tiny pieces of rock. Those pieces are called particles. And all of those

particles were once part of a bigger rock.

Rock does not break into particles quickly. Scientists say it can take

hundreds of years for just one inch of soil to form.

Many natural forces work to break rocks into particles. One is the sun. The sun heats the surface of rocks. This causes the outer layers to expand, or grow. At night, when the rock cools, it contracts, or shrinks. After numerous cycles of cool nights and hot days, the outer layers of rock break off. These pieces become part of the soil.

Ice also breaks rock into particles. Water seeps into the cracks of rocks. When the temperature drops to freezing, the water becomes ice. Ice takes up more space than water, so it causes the cracks to grow. Over time, bits and pieces of rock break off from these cracks.

21st Century Content

Scientists have discovered that the planets Venus and Mars have plenty of rocks on their surfaces. And natural forces such as wind break these rocks into sand and dust particles. But even with all of that parent material, these planets do not have soil like that found on earth. That's because a key ingredient is missing: life. Without living things to make **humus**, rock, sand, and dust cannot become soil.

Decaying plants form humus, one of the ingredients in soil.

Water and wind wear away at rocks, too. Rain, snow, and flowing water pound away at the outer layer of rock. Wind causes rocks to hit against each other. Bits and pieces of rock break away.

Living things break rocks apart, too. For instance, tree roots snake into rocks. This causes the rocks to crack, and particles of rock fall away.

Another ingredient in soil is humus. Humus is a mixture of the remains of dead plants and other organisms. It also contains the waste of living things that eat those remains. When plants and animals die, their remains decompose, or decay. Living things such as earthworms, fungi, and bacteria feed on the remains. Their waste then becomes part of the soil. Because plants and animals contain nutrients, these nutrients become part of the soil, too. This enriches the soil for future plants and animals.

REAL WORLD SCIENCE CHALLENGE

How do earthworms help make soil? To find out, wash out a two-liter plastic soda bottle and ask an adult to cut off the top just below the neck. Cover the sharp, exposed edge of the bottle with duct tape. Next, fill the bottle with alternating layers of moist soil and sand, each about 3 (7.6 cm) inches deep. Next put a handful of dead leaves on top. Place three to five earthworms in the bottle. You can get them from your yard or buy some at a bait shop or pet store. Place the bottle in a dark place. Water as needed so that the sand and soil stay damp but not too wet. Observe the worms every day. Write down what you see. How long does it take them to eat through the leaves?
(Turn to page 29 for the answer)

Particles of rock and humus come together in clumps. Between these clumps are spaces for soil's other ingredients: water and air. These are vital to everything that lives and grows in soil.

CHAPTER THREE

THE PROPERTIES OF SOIL

Some soil can support plant life, but some soil is too dry or rocky for plants to flourish.

Some soils are teeming with plants. Others have almost none. Some soils are dark and moist. Others are dry and gritty. The properties of soil determine what can or cannot grow there.

Many things affect the properties of soil. One is the soil's parent material. All kinds of rock can be parent material. Limestone is one common type. Limestone is soft and wears away easily. It is filled with minerals. Sandstone is another. It is harder but does not have many minerals. As these parent materials break into particles, the soil they make has the same properties as they do.

There are three kinds of soil particles. Sand particles are the largest. When they come together, there are large spaces between them. Water can easily drain through. Silt particles are the next largest. They feel like flour. The spaces between them are smaller than between sand. They hold some water and stick together when wet. Clay particles are the smallest. They have very little space between them, so water does not easily drain through them. Instead clay absorbs water and stays quite wet.

Most soils are a mixture of these particles. The amount of each affects the soil's properties. Plants do not grow well in soil that is filled with clay. Tightly packed clay particles do not allow roots to grow and

spread. Sandy soil is not good for plants either. Water drains too quickly

and easily through it. Soil with silt is good for plants. But silt is lightweight.

Wind or heavy rain easily carries it away.

REAL WORLD SCIENCE CHALLENGE

To find out how different soils hold water, use a toothpick to poke three or four holes in the bottom of three foam or paper cups. Spoon a different type of soil into each cup until it is about three-quarters full. You can use sand, gravel, soil from your yard or school, or potting soil from a nursery. Label each cup so you remember what kind of soil it contains. Pour a cup of water into each soil cup, letting the water drain into an empty cup below. Note how much water leaks out of each soil cup. Which soil held the most water? Which held the least? Which soil would be best for growing plants? Why?

(Turn to page 29 for the answer)

The best soil for plants has sand, silt, and some clay. This kind of

soil is called **loam**. It has large and small spaces for oxygen and water.

The clay keeps it from washing away or blowing away.

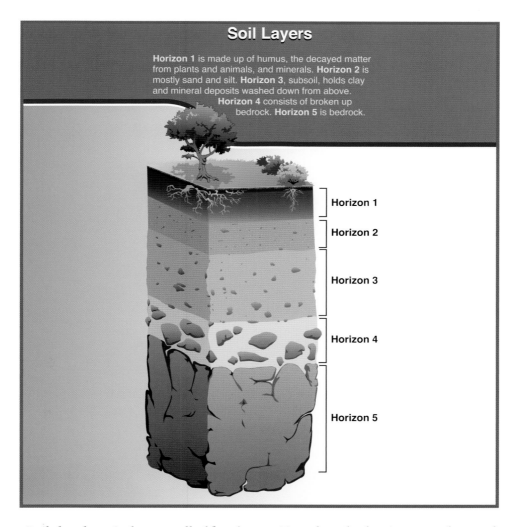

Soil Layers

Horizon 1 is made up of humus, the decayed matter from plants and animals, and minerals. Horizon 2 is mostly sand and silt. Horizon 3, subsoil, holds clay and mineral deposits washed down from above. Horizon 4 consists of broken up bedrock. Horizon 5 is bedrock.

Horizon 1

Horizon 2

Horizon 3

Horizon 4

Horizon 5

Soil develops in layers called **horizons**. Together the horizons make up the

soil profile. Topsoil is one horizon. It has humus and billions of living things

that feed on the humus. Topsoil is usually the darkest horizon and has the most nutrients. Subsoil is another horizon. It is lighter in color than topsoil because it does not have as much humus. There are not many animals or plants in this layer. The deepest horizon is the parent material, often called **bedrock**.

REAL WORLD SCIENCE CHALLENGE

You can see a soil profile in your own yard. Ask an adult to help you dig a hole in the ground. Be sure it is in a safe place where no one will trip on it! Make the hole about 12 inches (30 cm) wide and 12 inches (30 cm) deep. Now look at the sides of the hole. Write down what you see, taking note of different layers and colors. Draw a picture of the layers and label them. Next take a handful of soil from each layer. Rub it with your fingers. How does each sample feel? Is it gritty like sand or smooth like flour? Is it wet and sticky or dry? Place it on a piece of white paper and study it through a magnifying glass. What do you see in each layer? How big are the particles? Make a list of things you find, including worms, rocks, and plants.

(Turn to page 29 for the answer)

There are many different kinds of soil. And each kind has different properties. The type of soil that covers an area of land helps determine what plants and animals can survive there.

CHAPTER FOUR

SOIL LOSS

Water runoff has eroded the soil in this wheat field in Washington.

Soil loss is a problem around the world. When soil is lost, plants do

not grow. Animals and people who depend on those plants may suffer.

If the soil runs into rivers and streams, it can harm the water. Animals

and people who depend on that water may become ill and die.

Another word for soil loss is **erosion**. Erosion is any process that wears

away the surface of the earth. Erosion is a normal process. It does not always lead to problems. Some of the world's most beautiful landscapes

were created by erosion. The Grand Canyon is the result of erosion.

REAL WORLD SCIENCE CHALLENGE

You can see what soil erosion looks like for yourself. Do this activity outside, though, because you might make a mess! Cover the bottom of a paint tray with soil and rest it on a flat area of ground. Plant a few bean seeds in the soil. Next, fill a watering can with water. Then hold the watering can 6 to 8 inches (15 cm to 20 cm) above the soil and slowly pour the water onto the soil. Observe what happens to the soil and the seeds. Now hold the deeper end of the tray up about 4 to 6 inches (10 cm to 15 cm) off the ground so the tray is on a slope. Again, fill the watering can and pour the water onto the soil. What happens to the soil and seeds this time? How does this show you the problems of soil erosion?

(Turn to page 29 for the answer)

Water and wind cause erosion. When a hard rain falls, it can wash away the

top layer of soil, also known as topsoil. This layer of soil has the most nutrients.

This type of erosion is common in open areas where the land slopes. On a slope

with few trees or plants, nothing keeps rain from moving the soil downhill.

A patch of Brazil's tropical savanna, once lush and green, now looks dry and dead.

In dry areas, wind can cause erosion. Without water to hold the particles in place, dry soil is easily picked up by the wind and carried away. This happens most often in deserts.

Human actions also cause soil to erode. People cut down trees to make products such as paper. Trees are also cut down to create land for farming and grazing. When too many trees are cut down, it can lead to erosion. Trees help keep soil in place. The leaves keep some of the rain from falling to the ground. Tree trunks, branches, and leaves block

21st Century Content

Some areas of the world, such as deserts, are normally dry. But when land that normally gets lots of rain goes a long time without rain, it can be bad. This type of natural disaster is called **drought**. Drought does not occur all at once. It happens because of a lack of rain over several years. Over this time, the soil dries up. It becomes cracked and dusty. With no water to hold the soil in place, erosion becomes a serious problem. Plants that once held the soil in place can no longer grow. And the people and animals that depend on those plants die for lack of food. Drought is a problem in many parts of the world today. In Africa, for instance, millions of people are at risk of starvation each day because of drought.

the wind so it cannot easily lift the soil from the ground. Tree roots help soak up rainwater. Without trees, the water has nowhere to go. Once the ground is full of water, the rain floods the land and washes away nutrients.

Soil that is loose, moist, and full of nutrients is less likely to be affected by erosion. But over time, farming can take its toll on land. Many farmers use heavy machinery on their land. The weight of the machines presses down on the soil, closing the spaces between particles. Water cannot seep into the soil, so it washes along the surface, carrying topsoil and nutrients along with it.

Overuse by farmers and ranchers can cause soil to dry out and lose nutrients.

Some farmers overuse the soil. They grow crops in the same spot year after year. Or they allow animals to graze in an area for too long. Eventually the soil can dry out and lose nutrients. This leaves the soil at risk of erosion.

Erosion is a natural process. But too much erosion can lead to soil loss and big problems for plants and animals. Luckily there are ways to help prevent soil erosion.

CHAPTER FIVE

SAVING OUR SOILS

Soil that washes away because of erosion runs into and blocks waterways.

Farmers, scientists, and others are working to prevent and control soil erosion. There are things that you can do, too.

Farmers have ways to protect soil from wind and rain. They may change the shape of the land to control where rainwater goes. In areas where farmland is on a slope, farmers may create terraces, which look like steps. The terraces keep the water and soil from rushing straight down the slope. Some farmers plant trees on the edge of their land. Called

windbreaks, these trees keep soil from blowing away with the wind.

Farmers also control soil erosion by keeping the soil healthy. One way

farmers do this is by changing the way they grow crops. Some crops are

especially tough on soil because they use up all the nutrients. Other crops

are not as hard on the soil. Some even put nutrients back into the soil.

*Bean plants provide fertilizer for banana trees, a method that
allows farmers to farm and protect soil at the same time.*

Life & Career Skills

If this book has sparked your interest in soil, you might want to think about becoming a soil scientist. Soil scientists study soil. They help make soils healthier and prevent soil loss.

Soil scientists take on a wide variety of jobs. They can work for a government, university, or a private company. They might study soil in a laboratory. They might meet with farmers to help them improve their soil or prevent erosion. Or they might work in a state park to protect the land from erosion and protect visitors from falling rocks.

Soil scientists need to be trained in different areas of science and math. If you want to be a soil scientist, it helps to have a love of science and the outdoors. You should also have an interest in nature and an interest in protecting one of earth's most precious natural resources.

Farmers may grow one crop one year and a different crop the next. This is called crop rotation. Farmers may also add humus to the soil to keep it full of nutrients.

Scientists are looking for other ways to save soil. Some are studying a special soil found in the Amazon rain forest in Brazil. It is called terra preta, which is Portuguese for "dark soil." This soil was first made by ancient peoples. They made it from a mix of burned soil and straw. The result was soil loaded with nutrients and charcoal. The charcoal is what gives the soil its dark color. Scientists have found that soil rich

Compost (pictured) is made up of decaying plants that eventually turn into humus.

with charcoal supports large numbers of bacteria and other **microorganisms**.

These living things make the soil better for plant growth. Scientists hope to

re-create terra preta in other areas of the world that have poor soil.

You can help prevent soil erosion, too. One way is to make compost.

Compost is a mixture of plant matter that with time decays and becomes

humus. When you add it to garden soil you make the soil healthier for

all the creatures and plants living there. You can also reuse, recycle, and reduce: Reuse paper bags, recycle paper, and reduce the amount of paper you use. If everyone did these things, the demand for new products would lessen. Paper and lumber companies would then cut down fewer trees. This would then help prevent soil erosion.

REAL WORLD SCIENCE CHALLENGE

To create your own compost, fill a one-gallon zip-top plastic bag half full with a mixture of torn up leaves, grass clippings, bits and pieces of kitchen scraps such as fruit and vegetable peels, and torn up pieces of paper cups and napkins. Do not add any meat products (including eggshells), because they can cause harmful bacteria to grow. Next add a half cup (118 ml) of soil and one teaspoon (5 ml) of water to the bag. Seal the bag and mix all the ingredients together. Place the bag in a dark spot outside for two weeks.

After two weeks, notice any changes to the mix inside the bag. Then take your compost to your yard or garden. With a shovel, turn over the soil in a small area. Pour the compost onto the soil. How does your compost compare to the soil? Now mix the compost with the soil.

(Turn to page 29 for the answer)

Soil is more than the dirt beneath our feet. Soil is an important natural resource. It is an important part of life on earth.

REAL WORLD SCIENCE CHALLENGE ANSWERS

Chapter One
Page 6

After a few days, you should see all of the plants sprouting. As long as they get water, most seeds will sprout without soil. But the seeds that do not have soil will not continue to grow. Soil provides plants with the nutrients they need to keep on growing.

Chapter Two
Page 13

Earthworms can eat their own weight in leaves every single day. Depending on how many leaves and worms you use, it can take a month or more for your worms to consume all the leaves you have given them and to leave behind humus. Once they have, dump the contents of your bottle into your garden.

Chapter Three
Page 16

The type of particles in soil determines how well it holds water. Sand particles are large and do not hold water very well; the water will drain right through the sand and into the bottom cup. This is also true of gravel, which has even larger particles than sand. If the water drains through the soil from your yard quickly, it probably has a lot of sand in it. If the soil drains very little or not at all, it probably has a lot of clay particles in it. If it drains slowly, it may have a mixture of sand, silt, and clay particles. Gardening soil is made to drain water slowly so that plants can grow well in it. It has a combination of all three particles in it.

Page 18

Depending on the type of soil particles in the soil, you should be able to see at least two horizons— the topsoil and the subsoil. Notice how the layers become increasingly lighter in color as you look deeper into the hole. That is because the deeper you go, the less humus there is. The particles in the top layer are probably smaller than the particles you see in the deeper layers. You may find worms and other insects crawling around in the upper layers as well. In these layers, these creatures have more humus to feed on and oxygen to breathe. If the soil particles are mostly clay, the soil will feel sticky and you will be able to mold it just like the clay you play with. If the particles are mostly silt, it will feel soft and light. And if the soil particles are mostly sand, the soil will feel gritty and rough.

Chapter Four
Page 20

When you pour water over the soil on a flat surface, you may notice the water splashes on the soil. This may cause the soil to move or splash, which may unearth the seeds. When this type of erosion occurs on an area of farmland, the seeds may not grow. Left uncovered they may move with the water, get too much water, or dry up in the sun. When you pour water on the soil on an angle, the slope causes the water to carry the soil down the slope. This may uncover the seeds, carrying them along with the water and soil. Again, the seeds will not be able to grow.

Chapter Five
Page 28

After two weeks you may notice that the kitchen scraps you put in your bag are starting to break down, or decay. Tiny living things in the soil and air are responsible for making this happen. They feed on the dead plant matter and leave behind their waste. When you mix the compost with the soil, you may still recognize the scraps as pieces of plant material. The pieces are larger and coarser than the particles of soil. But over time, as more and more living things in the soil and air feed on the compost and leave behind their waste, the compost will mix in with the soil as humus.

Glossary

bacteria (bak-TIH-ree-uh) microscopic one-celled creatures

bedrock (BED-rahk) the rock, or parent material, that lies under the layers of soil

drought (DROWT) a long period of time with little or no rain and little water left in the soil

erosion (ih-ROH-zhun) the wearing away of rock or soil

fungi (FUNG-guy) living organisms that feed on dead plant and animal material

horizons (huh-RY-zinz) the layers of soil that make up a soil profile

humus (HYOO-muss) an ingredient of soil that is made up of the remains of dead plants and animals

loam (LOHM) a mix of sand, silt, and clay that is ideal for growing plants

microorganisms (MY kroh OHR gun izms) living things so small you need a microscope to see them

nutrients (NOO-tree-untz) substances that plants and animals need to help them to grow and survive

organisms (OHR-gun-izms) living things

oxygen (AHKS-ih-juhn) a gas that most living things need to breathe to survive

parent material (PAIR-unt muh-TEE-ree-uhl) the rock from which a certain type of soil forms

soil profile (soyl PROH-fyl) all the horizons, or layers, of soil that make up an area of soil

21ˢᵗ CENTURY SKILLS LIBRARY

For More Information

Books

Bourgeois, Paulette. *The Dirt on Dirt*. Tonawanda, NY: Kids Can, 2008.

Gardner, Robert. *Super Science Projects About Earth's Soil and Water*. Berkeley Heights, NJ: Enslow, 2005.

Lindbo, David. *Soil! Get the Inside Scoop*. Madison, WI: American Society of Agronomy, 2008.

Web Sites

Dig It! The Secrets of Soil
http://forces.si.edu/soils/
This site, sponsored by the Smithsonian Institution, allows visitors to interact with a live soil exhibit.

NASA's Soil Science Education Home Page
http://soil.gsfc.nasa.gov/index.html
This site offers everything you need to know about the soil beneath your feet.

USDA Natural Resources Conservation Service, "State Soils"
http://soils.usda.gov/gallery/state_soils/
Visit this site to find out if your state has established a state soil. If it has, what is it?

INDEX

ABOUT THE AUTHOR

Katie Sharp has written several books for children. She lives in Webster Groves, Missouri, with her husband, daughter, and son. Her favorite pastime is hiking soil-covered trails while exploring the beauty of nature.